Afro-Cuban Rhythms

Gig Savers Complete Edition

WWW.MELBAY.COM

CONTENTS

BIBLIOGRAPHY

Escuela Nacional de Artes Student Notebook, 1994

Personal notes from CUTUMBA Folkloric Group, Santiago, Cuba, 1998

Personal notes from AfroCubanismo Music Program, Banff, Alberta, 1994 & 1996

Santos, John "Conga de Comparsa", *Modern Percussionist,* March 1987 pp. 56-59

Garabaldi, David & Talking Drums, *Timba Funk,* Warner Bros. Publications, 1999

Malabe, Frank & Bob Weiner, *Afro-Cuban Rhythms for Drum Set,* Manhattan Music Inc., 1990

A special note of appreciation to Simone Manfredi and Virginia de Jong for proof-reading the text and to Mel Bay Publications for making this work available.

Trevor Salloum uses and endorses LP drums and percussion & Regal Tip Drum Sticks

INTRODUCTION

After numerous requests from my percussion students, I have compiled these volumes of Afro-Cuban rhythms suitable for a percussion ensemble. These rhythms have been notated in a convenient guide to facilitate the learning process and to save class time, allowing for more playing and less transcribing. However, no book can replicate the value of studying with a teacher, hearing live concerts or recordings of these rhythms.

Some of the best folkloric recordings have been made by the Cuban groups; Los Muñequitos de Matanzas, Afro-Cuba, Yoruba Andabo, Los Papines, Clave Y Guaguanco and Cutumba. I would encourage all students of Afro-Cuban music to obtain and study the recordings of these groups and many others. The recordings can be purchased through mailorder companies such as Descarga and Jazz Con Clave or through major retail outlets.

This guide is intended for intermediate to advanced levels with some reading experience. If one is not familiar with drum notation then a teacher is even more imperative.

Many of the rhythm patterns in this collection were compiled while attending “AfroCubanismo” in Banff, Alberta in 1994 and 1996 and field research in Havana and Santiago (Cuba) in the late 1990’s. Other patterns were derived and modified from the resources listed in the bibliography. Many variations exist for each of the rhythm patterns presented. These differences may be regional or due to individual interpretation. In addition, this collection is by no means complete but simply a starting point to tantalize the taste buds of those eager for adventure in the rich world of Afro-Cuban percussion.

Trevor Salloum
Kelowna, BC 2002

CLAVE - The name clave refers to both the instrument and the rhythm played by striking one hardwood stick against the other.

PALITOS - Sticks/ rhythm pattern played on the shell of a drum, piece of bamboo(guagua), wood or jam block

TRIAN/GUATACA - Metal hoe blade played with a metal striker

HIGH DRUM =QUINTO=SOLO DRUM=SALIDOR (in Conga style)

MID DRUM =CONGA=LLAMADOR=TRES GOLPE =SEGUNDO=MACHO

LOW DRUM =TUMBADORA=TUMBA=BAJO=HEMBRA =SALIDOR (in Guaguanco style)

STICKS =PALITOS=GUAGUA=CATA=KATA

( ) parenthesis suggests an optional stroke/note to be used at the discretion of the percussionist.

The quinto is the solo drum which is improvised and hence not transcribed.

All patterns are written in 3/2 clave but can also be started on the second bar to begin in 2/3 clave.

Drums are generally listed in order of pitch, starting with those of the highest pitch. Various sized conga drums (tumbadoras) can be used for all drum patterns although traditionally drums of different styles were used. The drums are usually played by hand unless otherwise indicated or notated with a stick symbol (+). All bell, guataca/trian (hoeblade), paila/guagua (kata) and pans (hierro) are played with sticks.

Note that throughout the book only the right hand (R) is indicated below the pattern, assuming the reader will understand that the remaining notes are played with the left hand. The placement of right or left hands is totally at the discretion of the player. Feel free to substitute a different combination of right or left sequence if it seems more natural to you.

The terms toe, touch, tap and finger tips can be used interchange-ably for the stroke executed by the fingers.

Throughout this volume when a muff/muted stroke is indicated it is played by striking the hand or stick against the head while muffling with the opposite hand. The muffling hand can press on the same side of the head as you are striking or the opposite head (if using a double - headed drum).

* Son · Mambo · Guaracha · Salsa

Son Clave

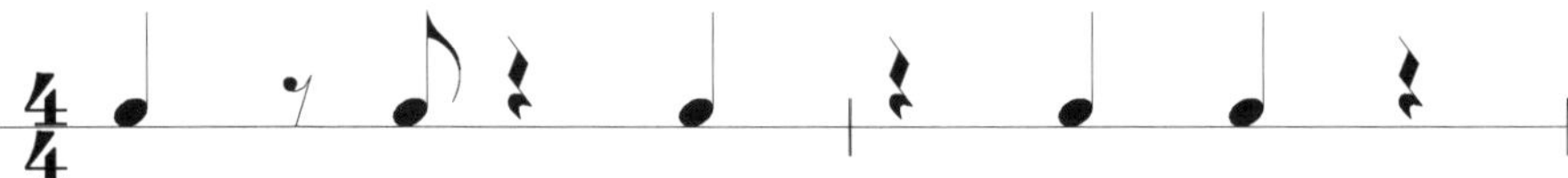

Tumbao/Marcha - One Drum
Conga

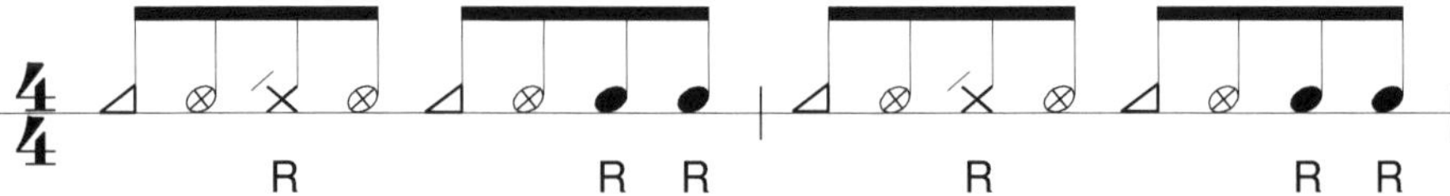

Tumbao/Marcha - Two Drums
Conga

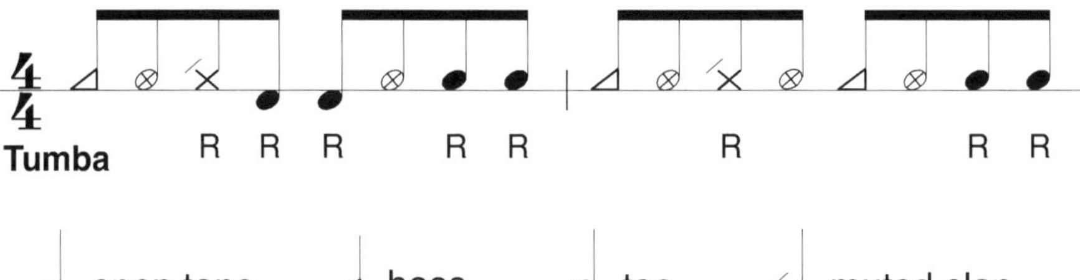

open tone   bass   toe   muted slap

*These rhythms would be considered popular rather than Folkloric, but I have included them because of their integral role in Afro-Cuban music.

Yambu (Matanzas)

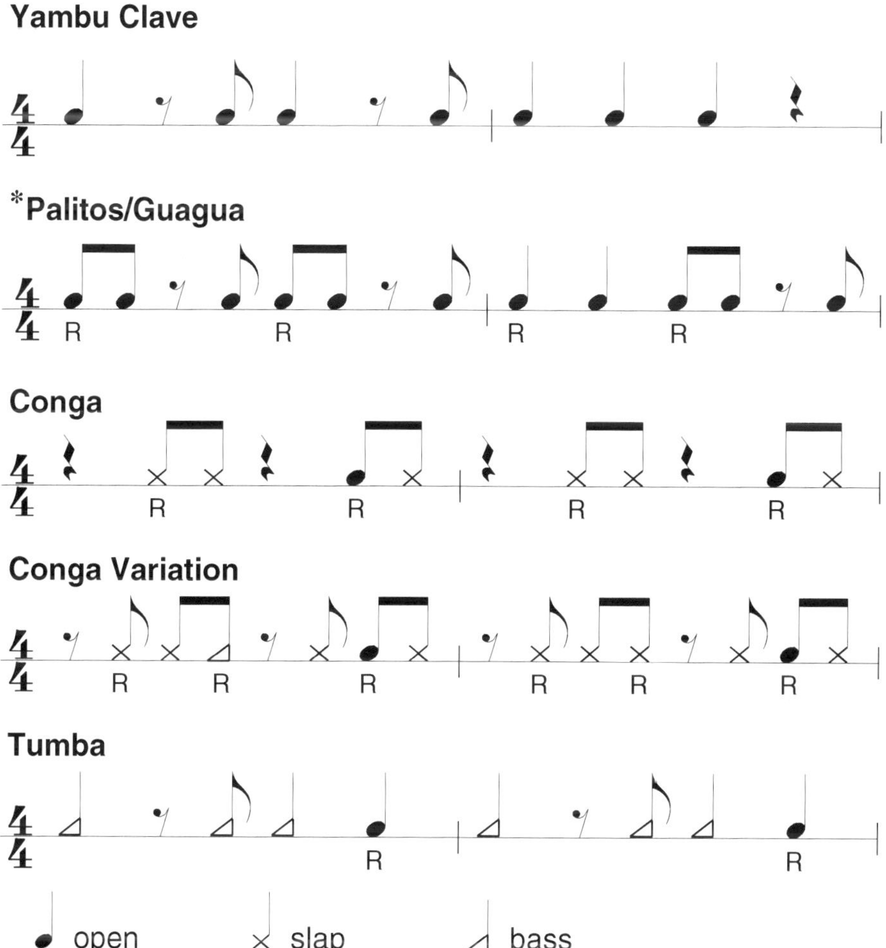

*Palitos patterns from guaguanco can also be used in yambu.

Quinto - improvises

Guaguanco (Matanzas)

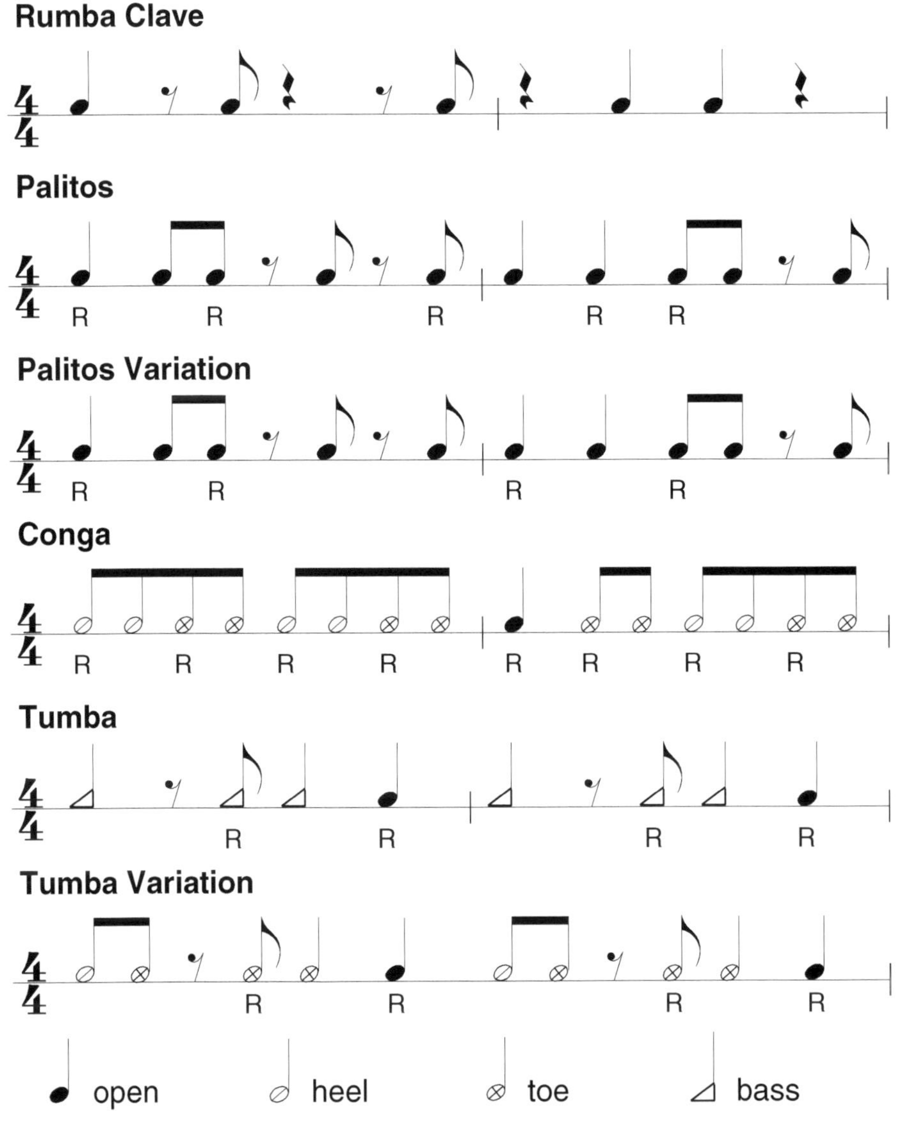

Quinto - improvises

Guaguanco (Havana)

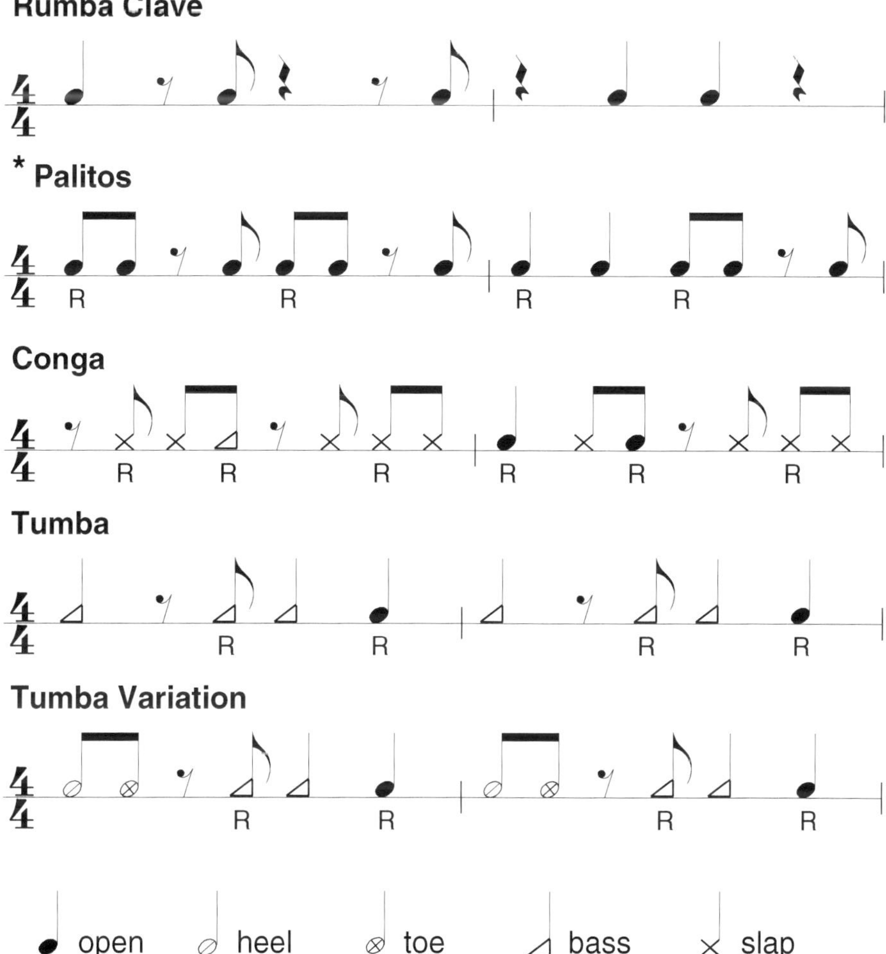

Quinto - improvises

* Palito patterns from Guaguanco (Matanzas) can also be substituted.

Rumba Columbia

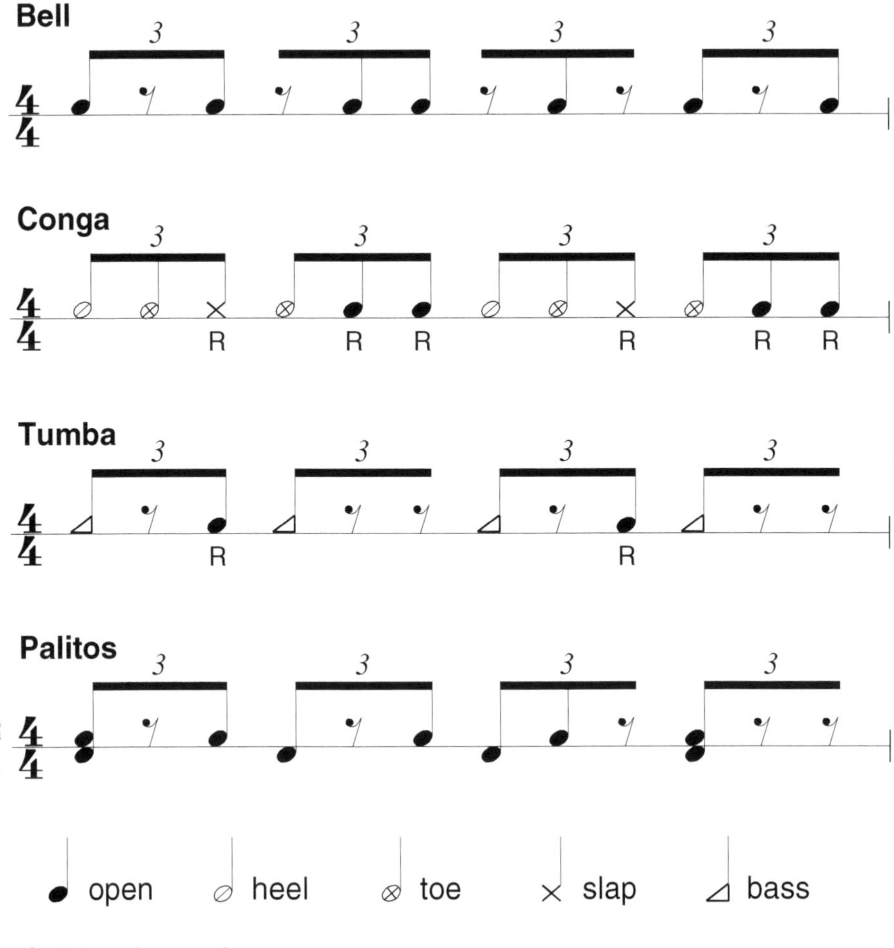

Quinto - improvises

Conga (Havana)

open slap

Conga (Havana) Cont'd

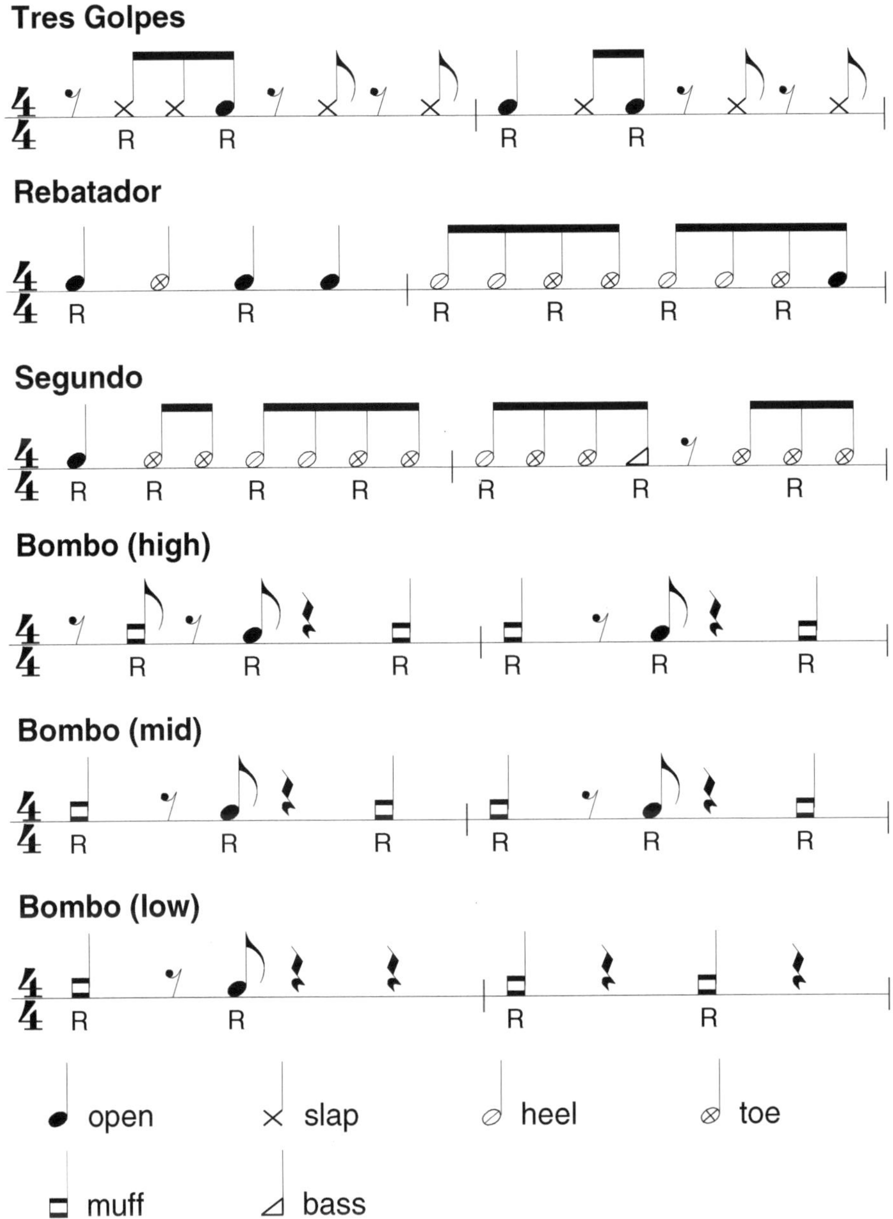

Conga (Santiago)

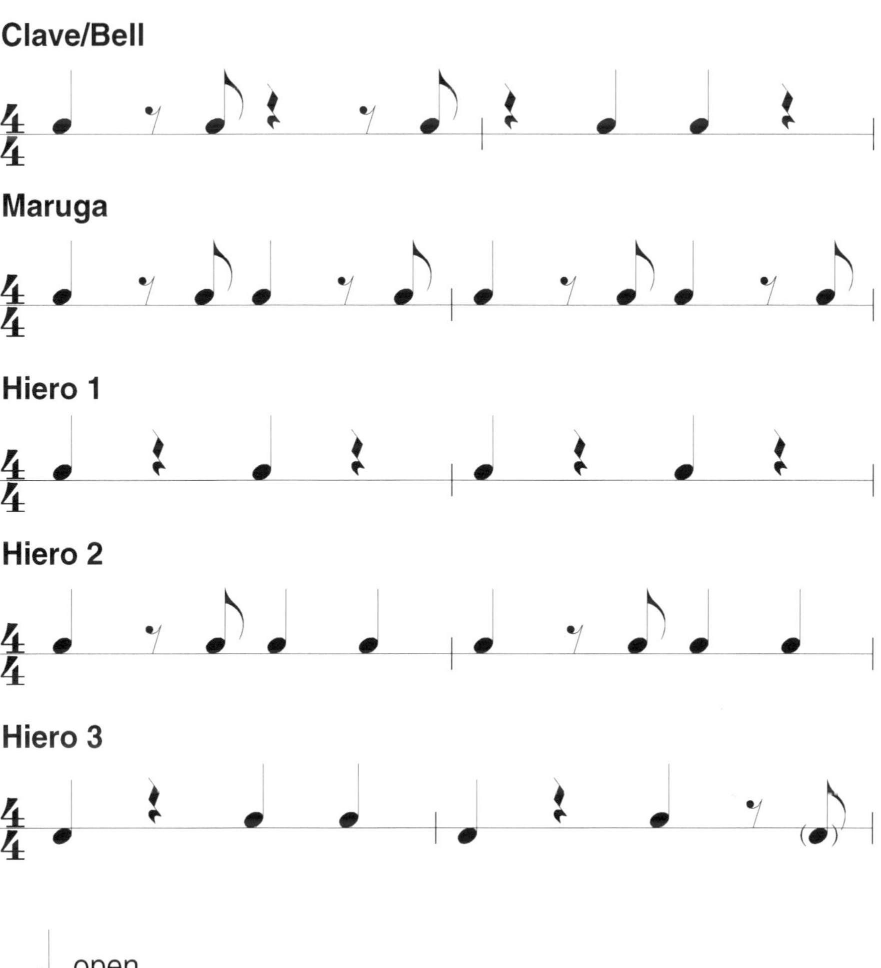

open

Conga (Santiago) Cont'd

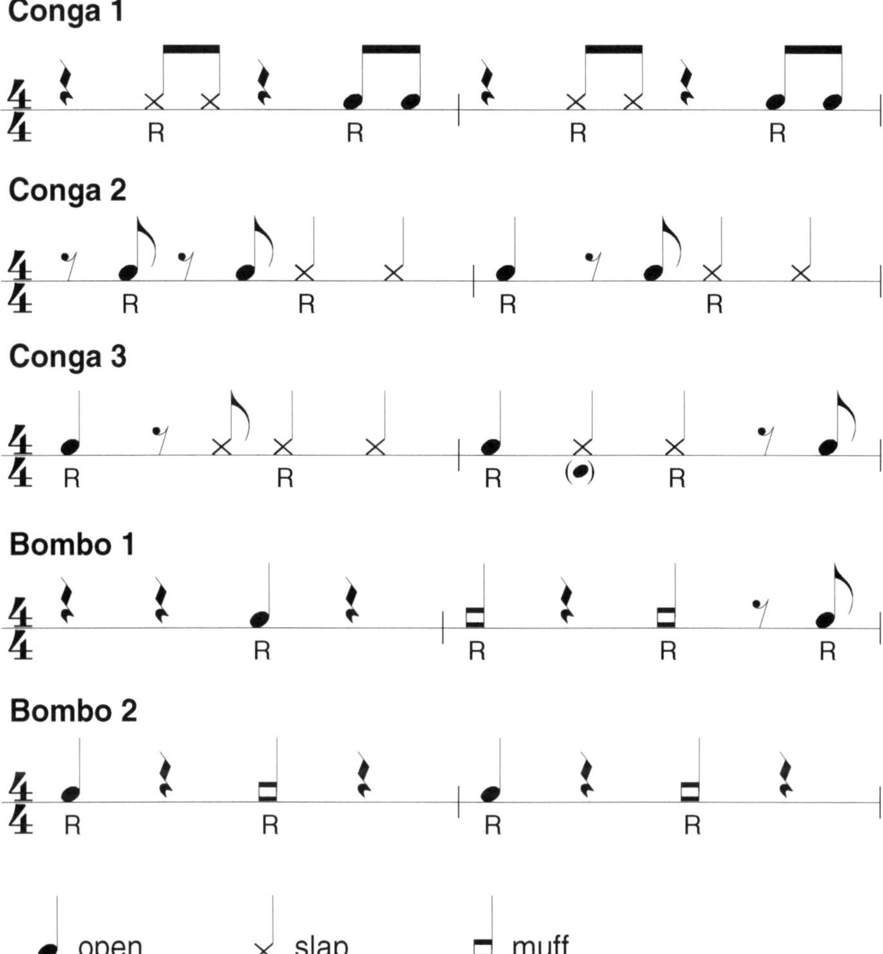

Conga (Matanzas)

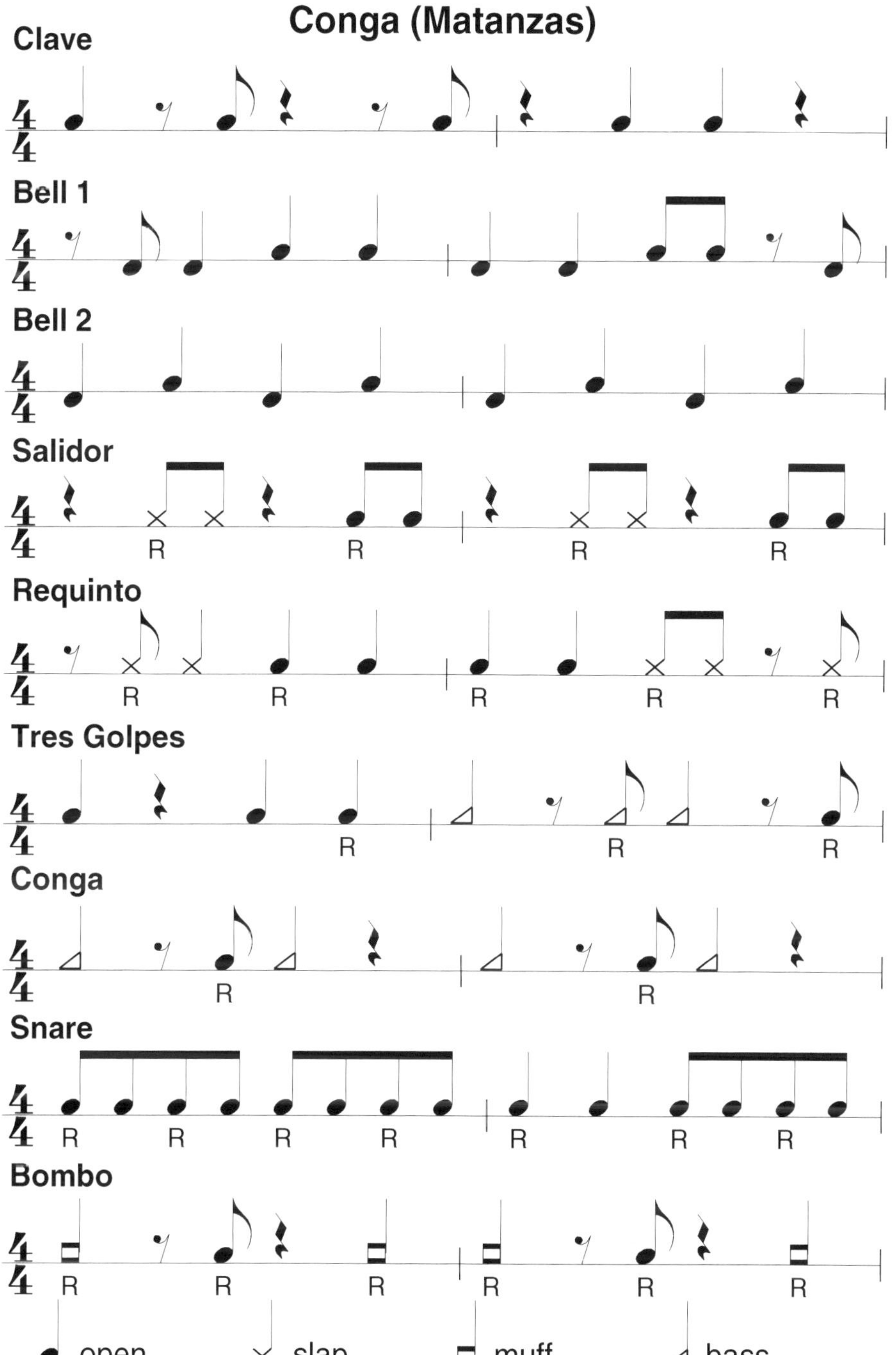

A BASIC GUIDE

CONTENTS

BIBLIOGRAPHY

Escuela Nacional de Artes Student Notebook, 1994

Personal notes from CUTUMBA Folkloric Group, Santiago, Cuba, 1998

Personal notes from AfroCubanismo Music Program, Banff, Alberta, 1994 & 1996

Askew, Greg "The Secret Abakua Society" *Latin Percussionist,* Issue 4, Summer 1996, pp. 10-12

Askew, Greg, "Tambores Iyesá", *Latin Percussionist,* Issue 3, January 1996 pp. 6-7

Garabaldi, David & Talking Drums, *Timba Funk,* Warner Bros. *Publications, 1999*

Malabe, Frank & Bob Weiner, *Afro-Cuban Rhythms for Drum Set,* Manhattan Music Inc., 1990

A special note of appreciation to Simone Manfredi and Virginia de Jong for proof-reading the text and to Mel Bay Publications for making this work available.

Thank you to Israel "Toto" Berriel, Jorge Ginorio and Scotty Wardinsky for providing assistance.

Trevor Salloum uses and endorses LP drums and percussion & Regal Tip Drum Sticks

INTRODUCTION

After numerous requests from my percussion students, I have compiled these volumes of Afro-Cuban rhythms suitable for a percussion ensemble. These rhythms have been notated in a convenient guide to facilitate the learning process and to save class time, allowing for more playing and less transcribing. However, no book can replicate the value of studying with a teacher, hearing live concerts or recordings of these rhythms.

Some of the best folkloric recordings have been made by the Cuban groups; Los Muñequitos de Matanzas, Afro-Cuba, Yoruba Andabo, Los Papines, Clave Y Guaguanco and Cutumba. I would encourage all students of Afro-Cuban music to obtain and study the recordings of these groups and many others. The recordings can be purchased through mailorder companies such as Descarga and Jazz Con Clave or through major retail outlets.

This guide is intended for intermediate to advanced levels with some reading experience. If one is not familiar with drum notation then a teacher is even more imperative.

Many of the rhythm patterns in this collection were compiled while attending “AfroCubanismo” in Banff, Alberta in 1994 and 1996 and field research in Havana and Santiago (Cuba) in the late 1990's. Other patterns were derived and modified from the resources listed in the bibliography. Many variations exist for each of the rhythm patterns presented. These differences may be regional or due to individual interpretation. In addition, this collection is by no means complete but simply a starting point to tantalize the taste buds of those eager for adventure in the rich world of Afro-Cuban percussion.

Trevor Salloum
Kelowna, BC 2002

CLAVE - The name clave refers to both the instrument and the rhythm played by striking one hardwood stick against the other.

PALITOS - Sticks/ rhythm pattern played on the shell of a drum, piece of bamboo(guagua), wood or jam block

TRIAN/GUATACA - Metal hoe blade played with a metal striker

HIGH DRUM =QUINTO=SOLO DRUM=SALIDOR (in Conga style)

MID DRUM =CONGA=LLAMADOR=TRES GOLPE =SEGUNDO=MACHO

LOW DRUM =TUMBADORA=TUMBA=BAJO=HEMBRA =SALIDOR (in Guaguanco style)

STICKS =PALITOS=GUAGUA=CATA=KATA

( ) parenthesis suggests an optional stroke/note to be used at the discretion of the percussionist.

The quinto is the solo drum which is improvised and hence not transcribed.

All patterns are written in 3/2 clave but can also be started on the second bar to begin in 2/3 clave.

Drums are generally listed in order of pitch, starting with those of the highest pitch. Various sized conga drums (tumbadoras) can be used for all drum patterns although traditionally drums of different styles were used. The drums are usually played by hand unless otherwise indicated or notated with a stick symbol (+). All bell, guataca/trian (hoeblade), paila/guagua (kata) and pans (hierro) are played with sticks.

Note that throughout the book only the right hand (R) is indicated below the pattern, assuming the reader will understand that the remaining notes are played with the left hand. The placement of right or left hands is totally at the discretion of the player. Feel free to substitute a different combination of right or left sequence if it seems more natural to you.

The terms toe, touch, tap and finger tips can be used interchangeably for the stroke executed by the fingers.

Throughout this volume when a muff/muted stroke is indicated it is played by striking the hand or stick against the head while muffling with the opposite hand. The muffling hand can press on the same side of the head as you are striking or the opposite head (if using a double - headed drum).

Bembe

Guataca (Hoe Blade)

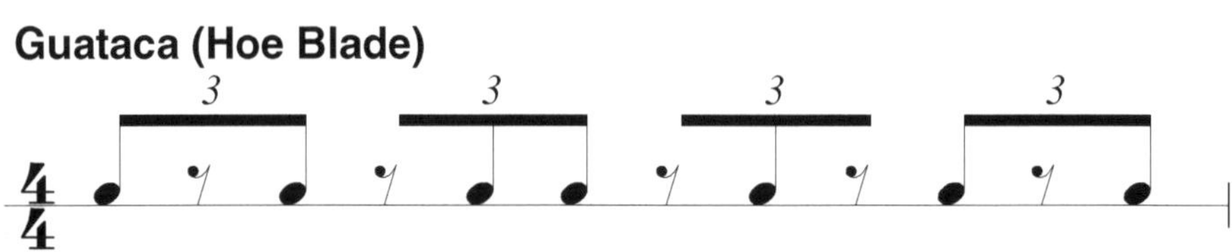

High Drum

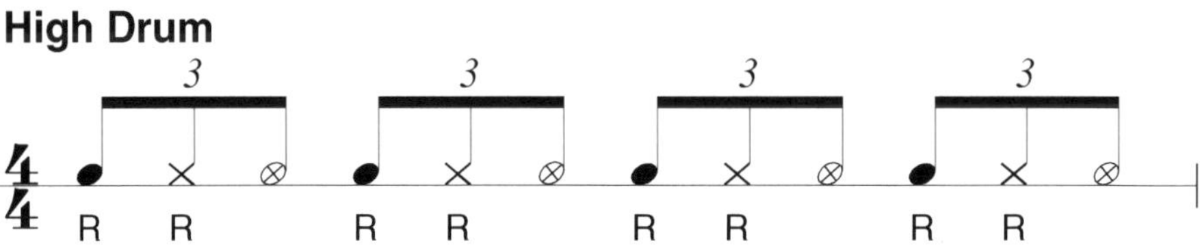

Mid Drum

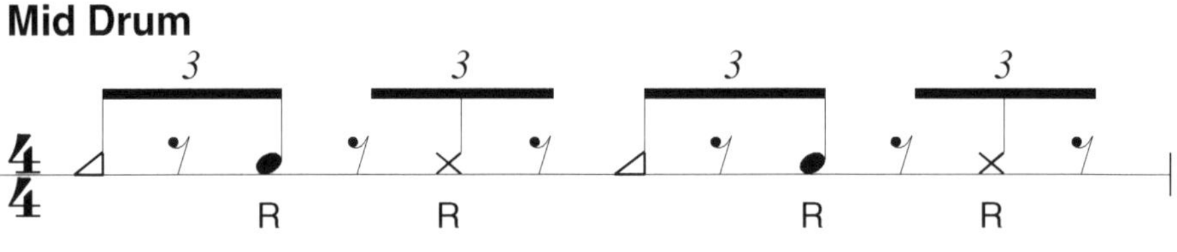

Low Drum

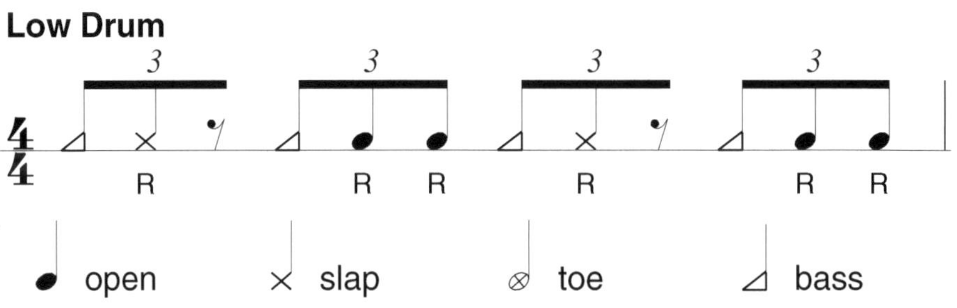

Makuta

Guataca

Kata (Palitos)

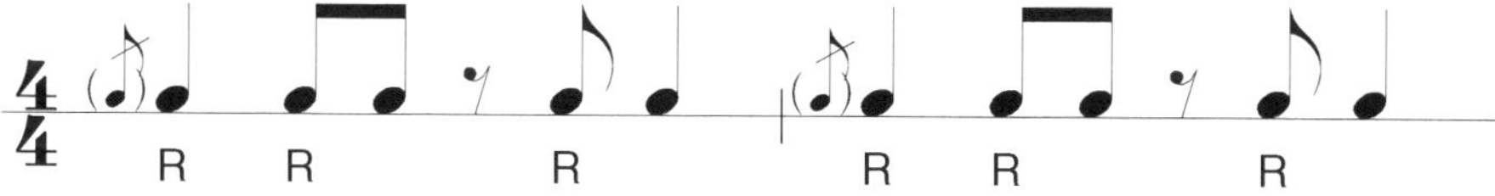

Cachimbo (High)

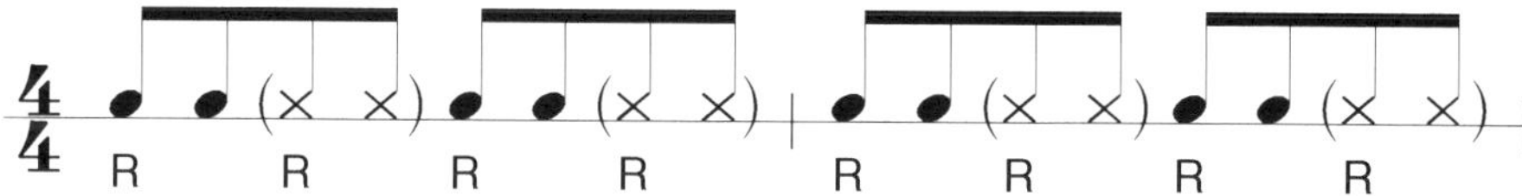

Mula (Mid)

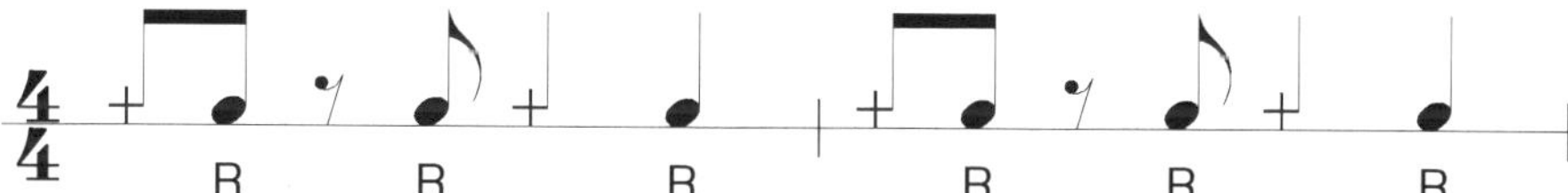

Caja (Low)

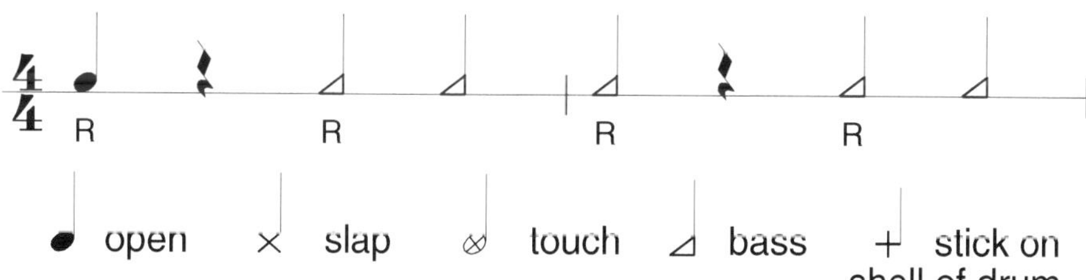

Yuka

Guataca

3 3 3 3 3 3

Cachimbo (High)

3 3 3 3

R R R R

Mula (Mid)

R R R R
L L L L

Caja (Low)

R R R

open

stick on shell of drum

bass

Palo

Guataca
Kata
R R R R
Cachimbo
R R R R
Mula
R R R R
Caja
R R R R
open
(with stick
for Caja)
slap
bass
toe
stick on rim

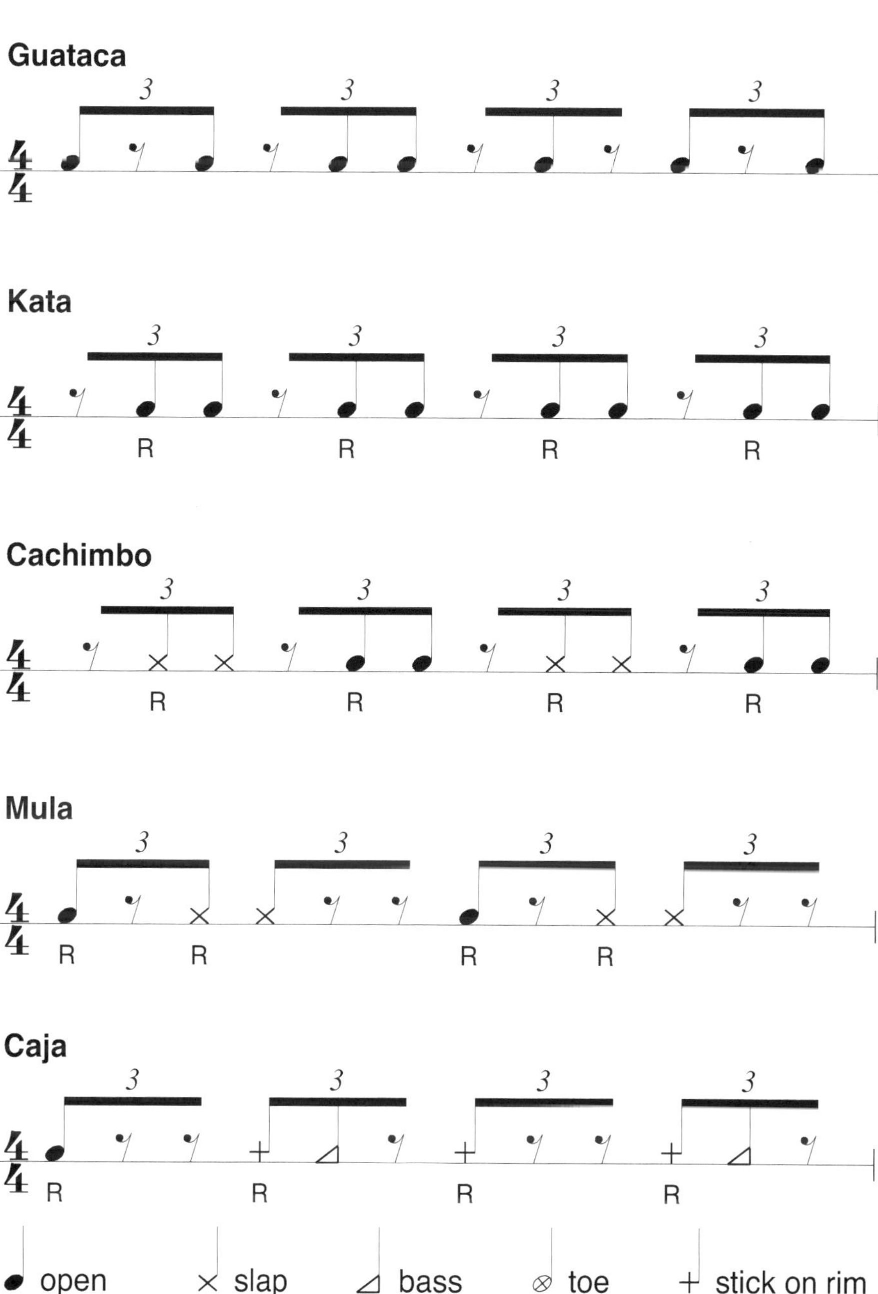

Arara

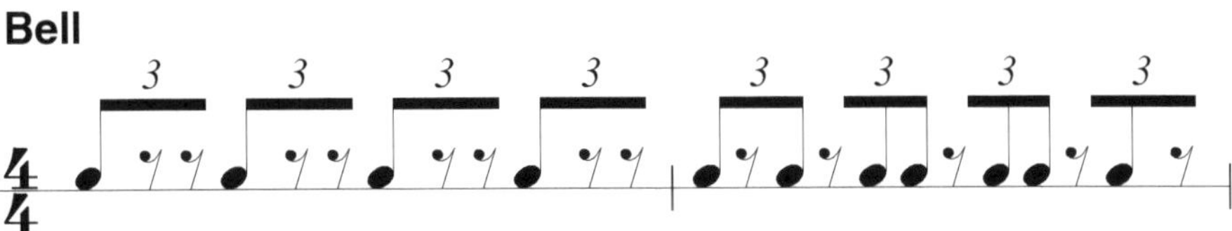

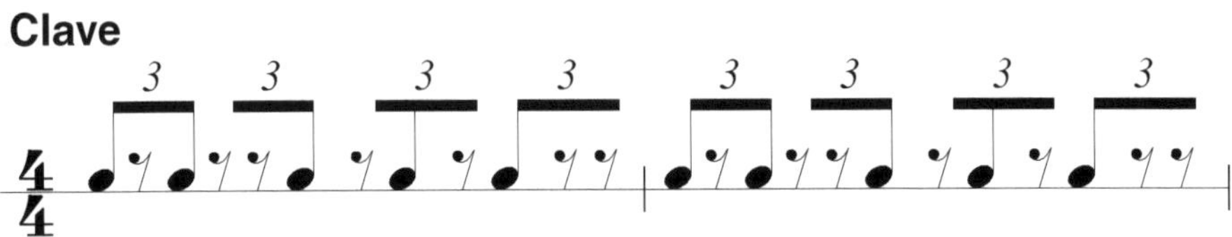

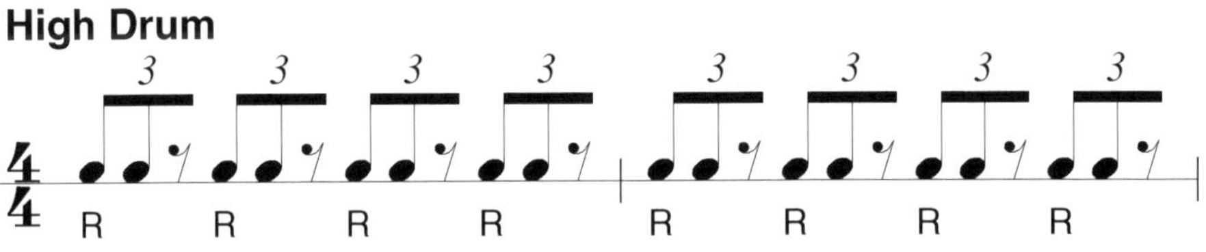

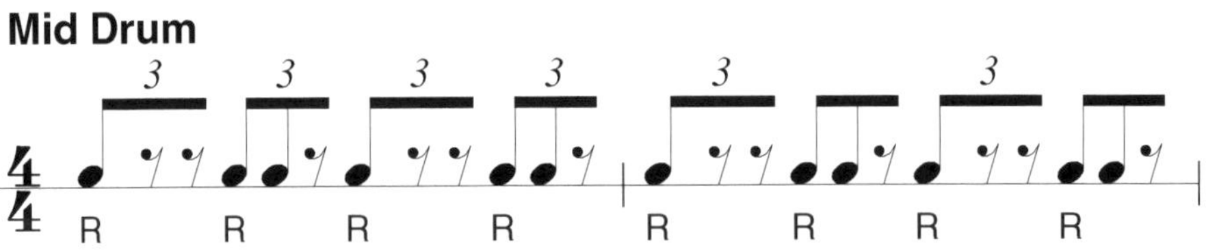

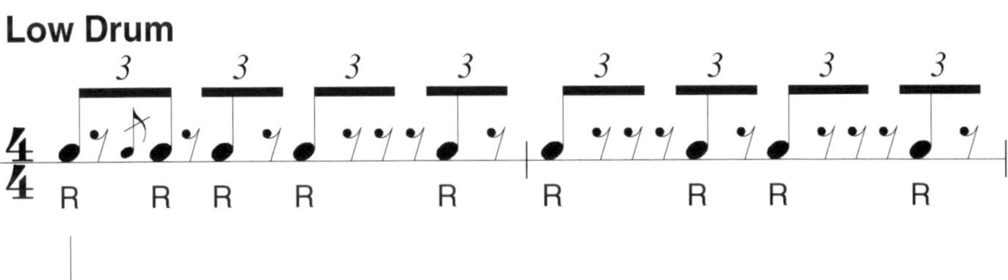

open

- All notes played with sticks on head
- Lead drum (not transcribed) plays with one hand and one stick

Abakua (Havana)

Ekon (Bell) 1

Ekon (Bell) 2

*Erikunde (Shekere)

R
L

Briankome (High)

R R R R

Kuchiyerema (Mid)

R R R R R R

Opiapa (Low)

R R R R

open muff

BONKO (Lowest pitch drum) solos

* ITONES (Palitos) play the same pattern

Abakua (Matanzas)

Ekon (Bell) 1

3 3 3 3

Ekon (Bell) 2

3 3 3 3

***Erikundi (Shekere)**

3 3 3 3

R
L

Biankome (High)

3 3

R R R R

Kuchiyerema (Mid)

3 3 3 3

R R R R R

Obiapa (Low)

3 3 3 3

(×) (×)
R R R R R

* ITONES (Palitos) plays same pattern
BONKO (Lowest pitch drum) solos

open toe muff bass slap

Gaga

Trian/Bell

Small Pandereta

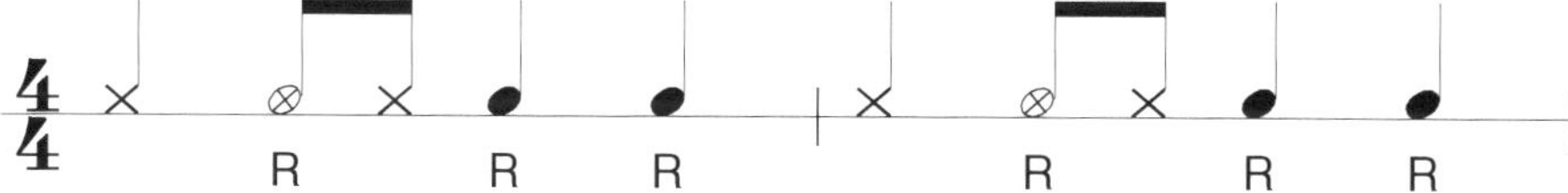

Large Pandereta

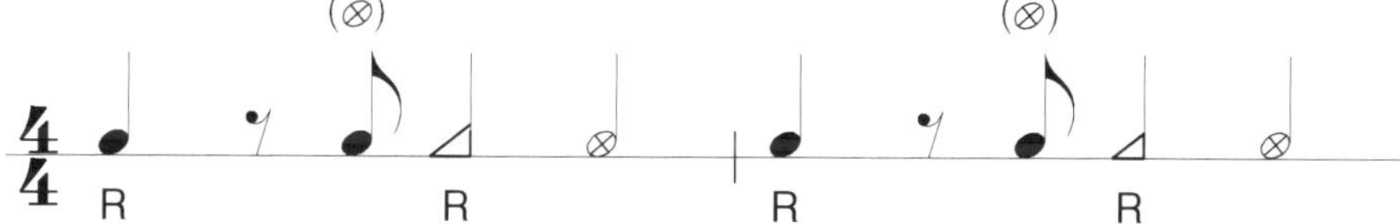

Variation (Small)

Variation (Large)

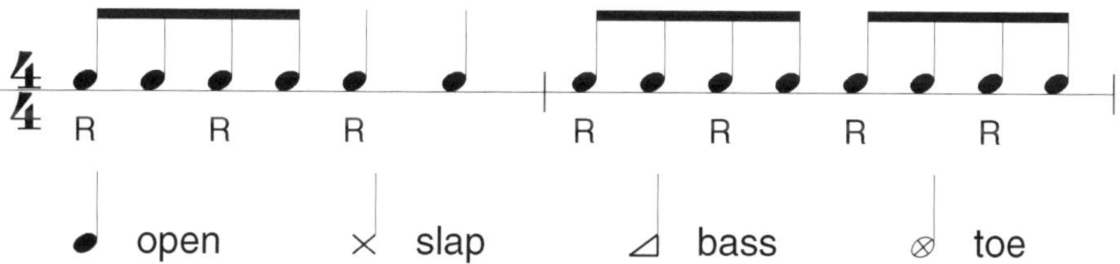

Vudu

Trian (Bell)

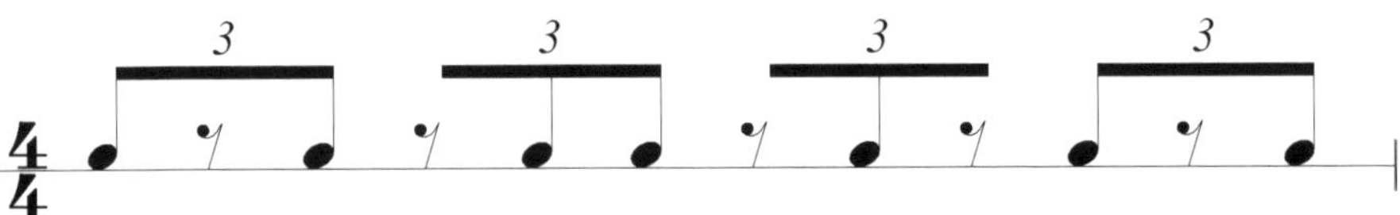

Egede (R + L play sticks on drum head)

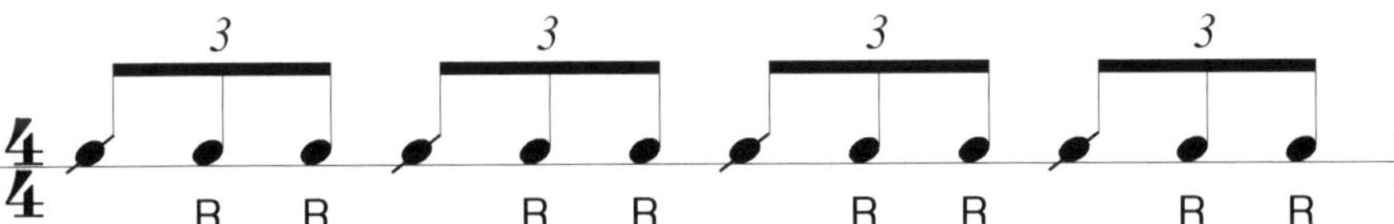

Sugo

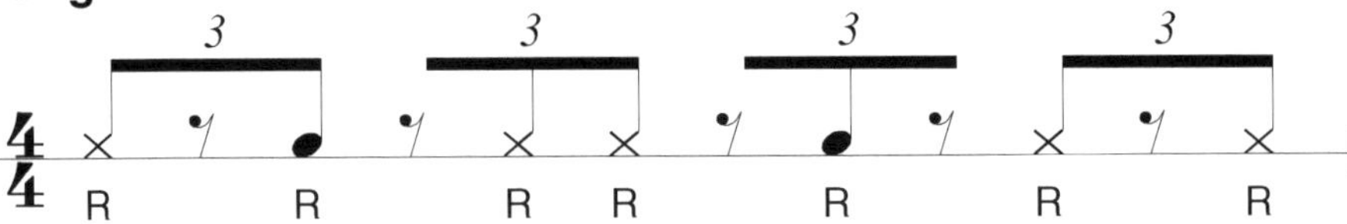

Rada (R.H. plays stick on drum shell)

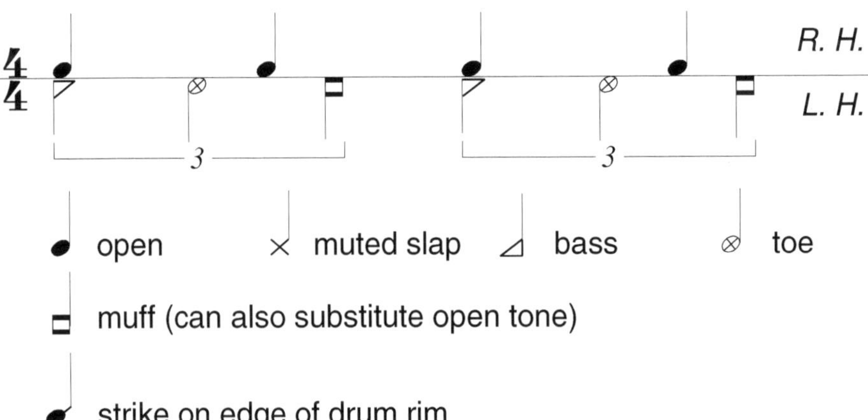

Iyesa*

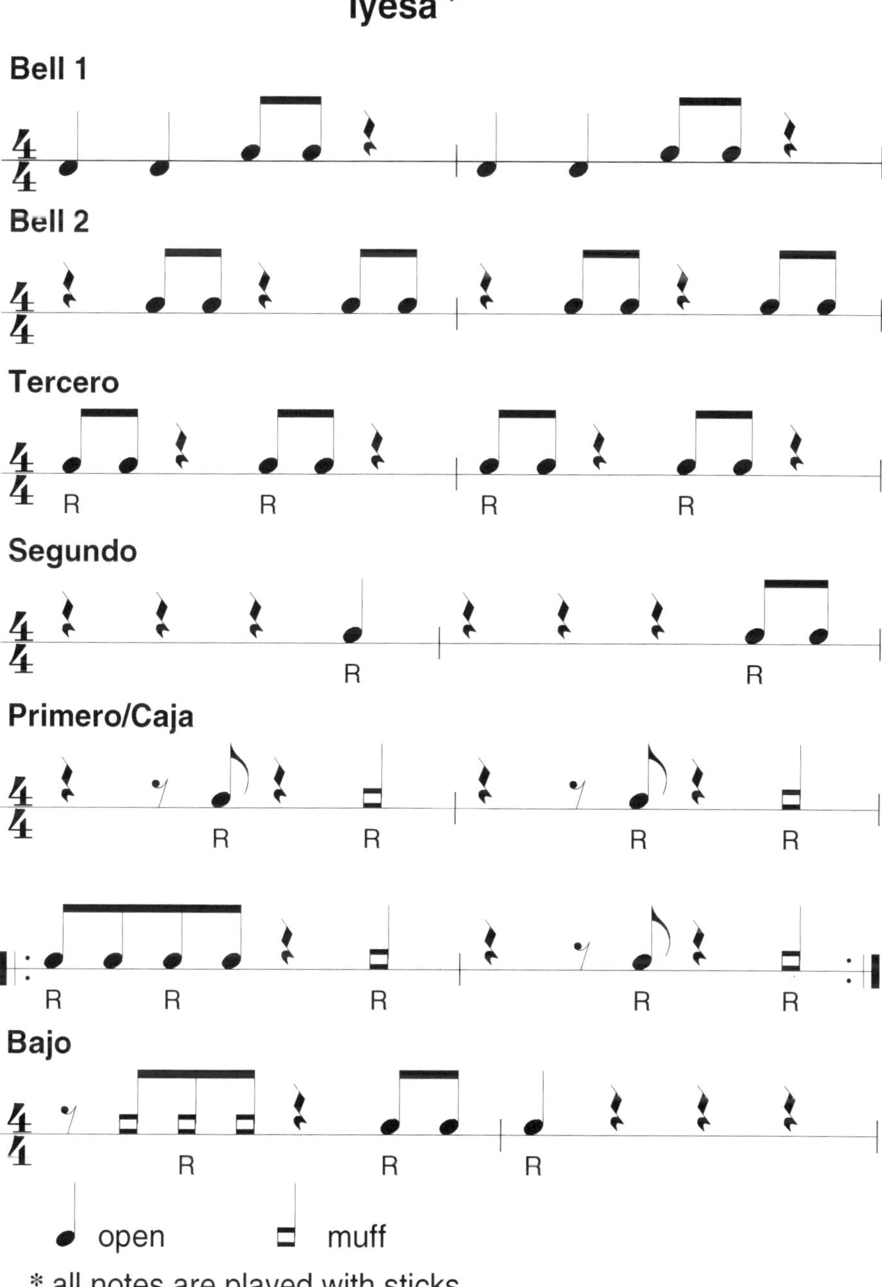

* all notes are played with sticks except the bajo which is played with "mano limpia" (clean hands)

About the Author

Trevor Salloum has studied with Cuban master drummers Changuito, Enrique Pla, Roberto Viscaiño, José Eladio Amat, José Miguel Meléndez, Cutumba and Los Muñequitos de Matanzas. He has made several trips to Cuba and studied at the prestigious Escuela Nacional de Arte in Havana in addition to music schools in Santiago and Guantanamo.

Trevor has played music professionally in Canada and the United States for over 25 years. He has performed with Pat Labarbera, Armando Peraza, Alex Acuña, Jane Bunnett, Campbell Ryga, Ross Taggart, Brad Turner, Dee Daniels, Tommy Banks and Ian McDougall.

He is a best selling author with Mel Bay Publications and his books include *Fun with Bongos, The Bongo Book, Bongo Drumming: Beyond the Basics* and *The Conga and Bongo Drum in Jazz.*

Trevor has taught percussion for over 20 years in Canada and the United States. Most recently he has been conducting Afro-Cuban percussion clinics as an artist in residence for the Vancouver School Board and for with the Britannia World Music Program in Vancouver, BC.

Made in the USA
Monee, IL
10 December 2021

84402799R00020